STAND THEREFORE:

A Practical Guide to Spiritual Warfare

SARAH R. ENTERLINE

Enterline Press
www.enterlinepress.com

Cover / Interior Design *by* Matt Enterline

Cover / Interior Art *by* Thiago Del Ponte

First Printing: April 2023

ISBN 979-8-9879332-0-6

TABLE OF CONTENTS

INTRODUCTION

I grew up in a Christian home, made a public decision to get saved at a Harvest Crusade at 7 years old, and got baptized with water at 10 years old. My dad was the head of the Ushers ministry and on the Board of Elders, so I was literally at church for every service of the week and any other event as well. I even started to volunteer in the nursery with the babies during the other services because I didn't want to attend Sunday school and hear the same lesson three times in a row.

When I was 13, I had the opportunity to go to a youth camp, and experienced being baptized in the Holy Spirit. To this day, I remember it vividly. During the afterglow, my youth pastor asked if anyone felt called to be especially set apart to serve God with their life. I was compelled to get up, went to the altar, and cried like a baby while the leadership prayed over me. Since that day, in many ways, my life has never been the same.

It has been different in good ways, as I felt the Lord change my heart and my attitude for the better (which, during middle school, was in desperate need of adjustment). I stopped wanting to please everyone else and started to care more about what God thought about my life and my decisions. However, what many people don't tell you is that when you step out like that, when you tell Jesus "I am all Yours, do with me what You will", Satan does not like it very much. Since that day (25 years now), I have had a very clearly-marked, spiritual target on my back. Do not believe the lie that everything is sunshine and roses once you become a Christian. Jesus promised if you follow Him, that means you follow Him in His trials and tribulations, as well as in the blessings. Now, any good Christian worth their salt will tell you that the eternal blessings outweigh the temporal sufferings, but that knowledge doesn't always make it easier in the moment, here on Earth.

Throughout the years, I have been attacked in every way possible, and have gone through many things I never thought I could survive. But God. Like a good Father, He doesn't leave us alone without help. In the Bible, He not only gives clear insight into the basics of this invisible battle, but also tells us how to fight it, and WIN. This little booklet is the product of all my years of study and teaching, as well as real-life experiences full of struggle and victory. Whenever I speak on this topic at conferences, I get asked for my presentation, so I figured I would just write it all out and have it ready to hand people when they ask for it. I hope it informs and encourages you, so that when you are going through trials or tribulations, you remember that you are not alone. There is a Helper backed by a heavenly host Who will do the heavy lifting. Just be still, and know that He is God.

May the Lord bless you and keep you,
May the Lord make His face shine
upon you and be gracious to you;
May the Lord turn His face
toward you and give you peace.
Num. 6:24-26, Paraphrase, NIV

~ *Sarah*

PART I:
THE BATTLE

"Finally, be strong in the Lord and in the strength of his might. Put on the whole armor of God, that you may be able to stand against the schemes of the devil. For we do not wrestle against flesh and blood, but against the rulers, against the authorities, against the cosmic powers over this present darkness, against the spiritual forces of evil in the heavenly places. Therefore, take up the whole armor of God, that you may be able to withstand in the evil day, and having done all, to stand firm."

Ephesians 6:10-13

1
WHAT IS SPIRITUAL WARFARE?

The phrase "spiritual warfare" refers to a battle that is constantly raging all around us. This battle can be described as spiritual, supernatural, or metaphysical, which are just fancy ways of saying the action is invisible to humans. It is a battle being fought between God's spiritual forces of good and the devil's spiritual forces of evil. "What does that have to do with me?", you may wonder. Well, YOU are literally the reason they are fighting, but we will get more into that later.

Just like gravity or the wind, you may not be able to see what is happening, but you will be affected by it. Therefore, we must be equipped to fight in the battle. "How can I, a physical being, fight against metaphysical forces, you ask?" Well, more on that later as well.

While this battle is invisible, the effects can be quite visible. You may be affected in many ways: spiritually, emotionally, mentally, or physically. Sometimes it manifests in more than one area at once. At this point, you may be skeptically scoffing and thinking that I am someone who sees a demon behind every bush. I can assure you I'm not. I recognize that we live in a fallen world and sometimes our circumstances are simply a result of sin permeating our habitation.

However, I also read the Bible and reside in reality. So, I recognize that there is a point where we cross the line from being a passive victim of fallen circumstances, to being actively attacked––to keep us from fulfilling the Gospel mandate given to us by God. At that point, it is time to get off the sidelines and get in the fight.

I know that can sound scary. The last thing to remember is that you are not fighting alone. In fact, victory in this battle can *only* come through the Lord! This is because you can do nothing in your own strength, but that is why God has the multitude of His heavenly forces at your disposal. Not only that, you have God

Himself. 1 Corinthians 3:16 says, *"Do you not know that you are the temple of God and the Spirit of God dwells in you?"*

Even when you feel alone, you need to take that lonely thought captive and remind yourself that *"God is our refuge and strength, an ever-present help in trouble, therefore, we will not fear… The Lord Almighty is with us; the God of Jacob is our fortress,"* (Ps. 46:1-11). Whenever I get anxious or fear for the future, just reading Psalm 46 brings great comfort and peace. As we will discuss more in-depth later, wielding the truth of God's word is an extremely effective strategy in this spiritual battle!

2
WHO IS ATTACKING US?

The Bible tells us that our adversary is the Devil, or Satan. The word **devil** is the English translation of *diablos*, a Greek word for "adversary", while **Satan** is the English transliteration of *satan* (saw-tawn) a Hebrew word for "adversary". Notice that "Devil" and "Satan" are not names, they are titles, he is the Adversary. "Well, of course," you think, "his name is Lucifer." Not so fast.

Isaiah 14 declares, *"How you are fallen from heaven, O **Day Star**, son of Dawn!"*

"Day Star", or "Morning Star", is only translated as "Lucifer" in the KJV. In the original Hebrew, it is *helel* which means "Shining One", which became "light-bearer" or "Lucifer" in the Latin. This is the only time it appears in the Bible, and since this was a choice by the translator of the KJV, we aren't necessarily sure if it was supposed to be translated as an official name, or just another title. Therefore, we don't actually know the name of our main Adversary.

Some people argue that his actual name is "Satan", and point to Luke 10:18. In the English, it would appear that it is being used as a name. The verse says,

And [Jesus] said to them, "I saw Satan fall like lightning from heaven."

However, remember that the Bible was not originally written in English, so we have to consult the Greek. In the original Greek it says *"Ton/ho Satan"* not just "Satan". This definite article indicates that there should be a "the" preceding the word Satan. It is a definite article that indicates specificity, so he is not just some general adversary, but THE main Adversary. So, while Jesus IS confirming the historical account of the fall of Satan for the hearer, He is NOT confirming a specific name. It should be more accurately translated:

And [Jesus] said to them, "I saw [the] Satan fall

like lightning from heaven." (Luke 10:18)

Due to habit (and for ease of reading), I will be using "Satan" or "Lucifer" like names for the rest of this little booklet, but the fact that we don't know his actual name makes him even scarier. What I mean is, because he is a deceiver and an angel of light (2 Corinthians 11:14), he can appear as whoever, or whatever, he needs to in order to trick us. The fact that he is an invisible attacker that can't be named, makes it way more difficult to defeat him. Do not underestimate him!

Revelation 12:9 describes him as a dragon: *"The great dragon was hurled down — that ancient serpent called the devil, or [the] Satan, who leads the whole world astray. He was hurled to the earth, and his angels with him."* It also describes him as leading the whole Earth astray through deception. Beware of his tactics! (More on this later.)

3
WHERE DID HE COME FROM?

First, Ezekiel 28 records a conversation God had with the King of Tyre, believed to be possessed by Satan. Genesis records that no one was in the Garden of Eden except for Adam, Eve, God, and Satan; certainly not a human king of a kingdom that didn't exist yet. Therefore, we must conclude that when God speaks of this "king" being in the Garden, He is addressing the spirit possessing the human, not the mortal king himself.

Verses 12-17 state, *Thus says the Lord God: "You were the [symbol] of perfection, full of wisdom and perfect in beauty. You were in Eden, the garden of God; every precious stone was your covering…*

You were an anointed guardian cherub.[1] I placed you; you were on the holy mountain of God; in the midst of the stones of fire you walked. You were blameless in your ways from the day you were created,[2] until unrighteousness was found in you. In the abundance of your [skill][3] you were filled with violence in your midst, and you sinned; so I cast you as a profane thing from the mountain of God, and I destroyed you, O guardian cherub, from the midst of the stones of fire. Your heart was proud because of your beauty; you corrupted your wisdom for the sake of your splendor.[4]"

We learn a few things from this passage:

1. Satan was a guardian angel of the rank cherubim in the Garden before he fell.

2. Angels are created innocent, but have a free will.

3. He was very talented.

4. Satan chose his appearance and beauty against his better judgment! He had the wisdom to know it was wrong and did it anyway.

Second, Isaiah 14 records the moment of Satan's pride and fall. God addressed Lucifer as he possessed the King of Babylon: *"How you are cut down to the ground, you who laid the nations low! You said in your heart, 'I will ascend* to heaven; above the stars [angels] of God, I will set my throne on high; I will sit on the mount of assembly in the far reaches of the north; I will ascend above the heights of the clouds; I will make myself like the Most High.' But you are brought down to Sheol, to the far reaches of the pit." (Isaiah 14:12-14)

Here we learn that pride led to Satan's fall. He wanted to be like God, but that was not his created purpose. Just like ours is not to be God.

Lastly, since he was cast out of heaven, Satan has been at work on Earth. In Revelation 12:4, it records the moment Satan realizes that God has a plan that has to do with the human race, and he decides to turn his focus to destroying them instead.

It says, "[the dragon's] tail swept a third of the stars [angels] out of the sky and flung them to the earth. The dragon stood in front of the woman [Israel] who was about to give birth, so that it might devour her Child the moment he was born."

Satan's whole goal is to destroy the human race.

Peter warns that "your adversary the **Devil** prowls around like a roaring lion, seeking someone to devour." (1 Pt. 5:8)

In Eph. 2:2, Paul describes Satan as "the **prince**

of the power of the air, *the spirit who now works in the sons of disobedience."* The word 'air' there means atmosphere, as in OUR atmosphere. This means he is here, influencing humankind to disobey God.

1 Jn. 5:19 states that *"the whole world lies under the sway of the **wicked one**."*

Later in Revelation 12:10, John calls Satan *"the **accuser** of our brethren... who accused them before our God, day and night."*

He is also continually working to cause division between the Creator and His creation. An example of this is the book of Job.

Job chapters 1-2 tell us that Satan has limited access to heaven and can come before the throne of God. Job 1:6-7 records that *"One day the angels came to present themselves before God, and the **Adversary** also came with them. God said to the Adversary, 'Where have you come from?' He answered God, 'From roaming throughout the earth, going back and forth on it.'"*

Notice it says they "presented" themselves before God. In the Hebrew, this implies servants presenting themselves to their Master to await instructions for service. Also, it is not just heavenly angels but fallen ones as well. This tells us that God is in complete control of the world – including Satan. The enemy must get permission from God to test His children. God calls his attention to Job, like a proud Father, and gives Satan permission to test Job, but he could not cause his death. Satan may be able to test and accuse us, but he is on a leash.

After reading chapters 1-2 of Job, people often wonder why God allows Satan to test us, or allows us to suffer through trials. Contrary to popular belief, the MAIN purpose of book of Job is not to answer why the godly suffer, or why bad things happen to good people. That question never actually gets answered by God in the end. The primary purpose of the book is to teach us that God is Almighty and in complete control. The word "Almighty" (Heb. *El Shaddai*) is used to describe God 31x in the book. The secondary purpose of the book is to teach us to be patient, and trust that God knows what He is doing, BECAUSE He is Almighty. For more information on why God allows trials in our lives, see the Appendix.

4
WHY IS HE ATTACKING US?

First, humans are the vehicle through which salvation is to come.

Genesis 3:15 says, *"I will put enmity between you and the woman, and between your offspring and her offspring; he shall bruise your head, and you shall bruise his heel."*

This is known as the protoevangelium — the first gospel, and the first Messianic Prophecy. The verse introduces two elements previously unknown in the Garden of Eden, elements that are the basis of Christianity: the curse on mankind because of Adam's sin, and God's provision for a Savior from sin who would take the curse upon Himself.

As God is talking to the serpent, He clearly promises that the offspring of the woman-- the nation of Israel that comes from Eve (who is a human)--was going to defeat him in the future. Remember the dragon waiting to kill the Child of the woman in Revelation 12:4? Before the Messiah was born into history, Satan would have tried to infect or completely destroy the human race in order to prevent this Messiah being born and his own future defeat, and we see that multiple times throughout OT History. Think of the Flood: there were no righteous people left on earth except for the 8 members of Noah's family. Satan had infected all but them (See Genesis 6:5). Also consider how often, and with what tenacity, he attacked the children of Israel specifically: Pharoah killing the Hebrew children, their slavery in Egypt, their various captivities throughout the time of the prophets, and then influencing King Herod to kill all the male babies at the time Jesus was born. This doesn't even cover all of the persecution of the Jews and anti-Semitism that has occured in history since then!

The bruising of the heel in Genesis 3 is considered foreshadowing of the crucifixion, where Satan gets to inflict some pain on this Messiah, but in the end, is actually defeated himself at the resurrection when it turns out to only be a flesh wound, literally.

This leads us to understand that he hates us because he lost the ultimate battle and a HUMAN was the reason why. Revelation 12:11 and 13:8 explain that he was triumphed over by the blood of the Lamb slain before the foundation of the world.

1 Corinthians 15 says, *"The first man Adam became a living being; the last Adam became a life-giving spirit...The first man was from the earth, a man of dust; the second man is from heaven... Death is swallowed up in victory. O death, where is your victory? O death, where is your sting?...But thanks be to God, who gives us the victory through our Lord Jesus Christ."*

Jesus is fully human, yet defeated Satan at the resurrection.

John 10:10 *"The **thief** comes only to steal and kill and destroy."* Notice this is the opposite of Jesus' mission which is to come and give life, and life more abundantly.

Second, humans are made in God's image.

Satan wanted to be God! Isaiah 14 says that he stated he wanted to be like the Most High. How it must bug him that we were created in God's image! We are a constant reminder of the one thing he couldn't achieve.

Genesis 1:26-27 states,

Then God said, "Let us make man in our image, after our likeness. And let them have dominion over the fish of the sea and over the birds of the heavens and over the livestock and over all the earth and over every creeping thing that creeps on the earth." So God created man in his own image, in the image of God he created him; male and female he created them.

Third, humans can be forgiven.

Hebrews 2:14-16 *"Since therefore the children share in flesh and blood, [Jesus] likewise partook of the same things, that through death he might destroy the one who has the power of death, that is, the devil, and deliver all those who through fear of death were subject to lifelong slavery. **For surely it is not angels that he helps**, but he helps the offspring of Abraham."*

Angels are not eligible for salvation because they are immortal. They have free will, but their choices are permanent. Satan has no chance at being forgiven.

1 Peter 1:10-12 states that, *The prophets of old did their utmost to discover and obtain the salvation of souls…It is these very matters which have been made plain by those who preached the Gospel to you… – matters which angels desire to look into.* (My own paraphrase.)

Angels are not omniscient or all-knowing. They don't know all of God's plans, and are watching them unfold in real-time as we are. After Adam sinned, they were probably confused as to how God was going to fix what happened.

In Luke 15:10, Jesus states, *"Just so, I tell you, there is joy before the angels of God over one sinner who repents."* As mentioned above, angels can't see the future, therefore they don't know who will be saved and who won't. That's why there is a celebration whenever someone is saved. Satan is an angelic being and unless he has read Revelation, doesn't know he loses in the end. If he has read it, and knows he will lose, he will try to take as many people down with him as possible, just to stick it to God.

The next question at hand is how is he trying? Or more specifically…

5
HOW DOES HE ATTACK US?

Satan uses many, many tactics to attack us, or schemes as it says in Ephesians 6, but there are a few specific ones that I am going to cover here: Temptation, Deception, and Pride.

This threefold strategy comes straight from the Garden and is what Satan has been doing since the beginning, in one form or another. If we can recognize it, we will be less likely to be deceived by it.

Genesis 3:1-5 *"Now the serpent was more crafty than any other beast of the field that the Lord God had made. He said to the woman, 'Did God actually say, "You shall not eat of any tree in the garden"?'*

And the woman said to the serpent, 'We may eat of the fruit of the trees in the garden, but God said, "You shall not eat of the fruit of the tree that is in the midst of the garden, neither shall you touch it, lest you die." But the serpent said to the woman, 'You will not surely die. For God knows that when you eat of it your eyes will be opened, and you will be like God, knowing good and evil.'"

Wait, did Eve ever claim to want to be like God? Wasn't that what Lucifer wanted?

You see, the first thing Satan does is call Eve's attention to something she does not (and should not) have, and then gives her a reason why she should want it. This is known as…

TEMPTATION

Temptation is the consideration of denying God's will and giving into your own will.

This is Satan's first tactic: to get you to DESIRE something badly enough to be willing to DENY GOD instead of your own flesh.

How does he do this?

He directs your attention towards something you don't have, don't need, or shouldn't have.

How do we fight this?

1. *"The night is nearly over, and the daylight is*

near, so let us discard the deeds of darkness and put on the armor of light. Let us walk with decency, as in the daylight, not in carousing and drunkenness; not in sexual impurity and promiscuity; not in quarreling and jealousy. But put on the Lord Jesus Christ, and make no plans to satisfy the fleshly desires." Romans 13:12-14

So first, don't be like the rest of the world, flaunting your sexual desires and nature out in public. When you are living a life of sexuality that is against what the Bible teaches, you are spitting in God's face, especially when you parade it in the street. We are to deny ourselves until we are able to exercise that part of us appropriately in a marriage relationship.

2. *"Whatever is true, honorable, just, pure, lovely, commendable – if there is any moral excellence and if there is any praise – dwell on these things"* Phil. 4:8

Second, make a choice to stop listening to music, watching movies or T.V., or reading books that have zero commendable qualities. If you would be embarrassed to watch it with Jesus, you probably shouldn't be watching it.

3. *"For the weapons of our warfare are not carnal* [physical] *but mighty in God for pulling down strongholds, casting down arguments and every high thing that exalts itself against the knowledge*

of God, bringing every thought into captivity to the obedience of Christ..." 2 Cor. 10:4-5

When a thought enters my mind that is ungodly, I actually talk to God. I literally say in my mind, "Lord, take that thought captive." And you know what? After doing it a few times, it works every time. But it is my choice to call on God for help, or to let that thought take root in my mind. So third, take every thought captive to obey Christ!

Back to Genesis 3:1.

"Now the serpent was more crafty than any other beast of the field that the Lord God had made. He said to the woman, 'Did God actually say, "You shall not eat of ANY tree in the garden"?'"

No! God said they could eat of EVERY tree except one, so here he is twisting God's words. This is...

DECEPTION

Deception is portraying falsehood as fact.

This is Satan's second tactic: to get you to DOUBT God's word, and question everything you know to be true.

How does he do this?

After he directs your attention to what you

want, he convinces you that God would want you to have it, regardless of what the Bible says. I mean, God is a God of love, right? If He loves you, He wants you to be happy, right? Doesn't God say "Be happy as I am happy?" No!

"[Since] He who called you is holy, you also be holy in all your conduct, since it is written, 'You shall be holy, for I am holy.'" Sometimes things that make us temporarily happy or give us a boost of dopamine ultimately aren't good for us, or they don't make us holy.

Now, the Bible does teach that God is love, however, often when we love someone, that means doing what is best for them, in spite of what they want. The Bible says that the Lord chastens those whom He loves, (Heb. 12:6).

Think of it from a parent's perspective. We have kids that want to touch hot stoves, jump into pools before they know how to swim, and run into the street to get their ball without looking both ways. Are we going to let them do those things just so they "perceive" us to be loving parents? NO! No parent in their right mind lets their kid do whatever they want just so they will "like" them. We do what's RIGHT for them, despite how they "feel" about it.

How do we fight this?

Know your Bible SO WELL that unlike with Eve, Satan can't twist Scriptures to convince you that God is saying something He is not. An example of this is in Matthew chapter 4. When Jesus was being tempted by Satan in the wilderness, do you know how he fought him? With the word of God. That is why it is called our sword.

*"The tempter approached Him and said, 'If You are the Son of God, tell these stones to become bread. 'But He answered, "**It is written**…"*

However, Satan knows the Bible too, he literally tried to twist it to use against Jesus!

*"Then the Devil took Him to the holy city, had Him stand on the pinnacle of the temple, and said to Him, 'If You are the Son of God, throw Yourself down. **For it is written**…' "*

But Jesus saw straight through this tactic.

*"Jesus told him, '**It is ALSO written:** Do not test the Lord your God.' And [the Devil] said to Him, 'I will give You all these things if You will fall down and worship me.' Then Jesus told him, 'Go away Satan! For it is written: Worship the Lord your God, and serve only Him.'"*

So again, know your Bible so well Satan can't twist it to convince you it says what it does not. Second, literally tell Satan to get lost. Even if you need to say it out loud, do it. Those words have power when backed up by the mighty host of God!

Lastly, the third tactic Satan uses is...

PRIDE

Pride (according to the Bible) is the consideration of yourself above God and others.

Satan influences you to decide you determine your own truth and DEIFY yourself. Meaning you put yourself above God. You are now the god of your life, not Him. You think, "What does God want? Who cares, I decide my own truth."

How does Satan get you to that place?

Once he directs your attention toward something you don't have, he deceives you into thinking you should have it, and then tells you that you DESERVE it because of how amazing you are.

How many times do we see the slogan nowadays "Live your own truth"? No! Live God's truth! Your truth is inferior compared to His.

How do we fight this?

2 Tim. 4:3-4 *"For the time is coming when people will not endure sound teaching, but having itching ears they will accumulate for themselves teachers to suit their own passions, and will turn away from listening to the truth and wander off into [untruth]."*

My first piece of advice is to not live in an echo chamber! Make sure you surround yourself with accountability: people who (in love) will tell you when you are wrong and direct you to the truth. When you only surround yourself with people that agree with you, there is no iron sharpening iron happening. You will quickly become dull and useless, which is right where Satan wants you.

I'm going to be honest with you, if you don't have spiritual warfare happening in your life, you should be doing some heart examining, because the only Christians Satan doesn't attack are the ineffective ones that aren't a threat to him or his mission.

Proverbs 16:5 *"Everyone who is arrogant in heart is an abomination to the Lord; be assured, he will not go unpunished."*

My second piece of advice is to be aware that the Bible declares a punishment at the end for those who consider themselves immune from His will. Be HUMBLE!

"Pride goes before destruction, and a haughty spirit before a fall… There is a way that seems right to a man, but its end is the way to death." (Prov. 16:18, 25)

Take Satan as an example. Pride was his sin, and will be his fall. Revelation 12:7-9 chronicles the great future battle in heaven where Satan loses.

"…War broke out in heaven. Michael and his angels fought against the dragon, and the dragon and his angels fought back. But the dragon was not strong enough, and they lost their place in heaven. The great dragon was hurled down – that ancient serpent called the devil, or Satan, who leads the whole world astray. He was hurled to the earth, and his angels with him."

My last piece of advice here is have a healthy fear of God:

"By the fear of the Lord one turns away from evil. When a man's ways please the Lord, he makes even his enemies to be at peace with him… Whoever gives thought to the Word will discover good, and blessed is he who trusts in the Lord." (Proverbs 16:6-7, 20)

This does not mean we need to be afraid of God, but to have a reverence for who He is and give Him the respect He deserves. He created the world and its rules, and we need to honor the moral code He has set forth. We don't decide what is good or evil, that has already been determined. We just need to recognize them for what they are and trust that God as Creator and Judge knew what He was doing. Giving thought to the Word means using the Bible as our guide for godly living: to know what is good and to turn away from evil, which will ultimately please the Lord.

6

NOW WHAT?

Now, you go on defense.
You put on the armor, and you stand!

PART 2:
THE ARMOR

"STAND THEREFORE, having fastened on the belt of truth, and having put on the breastplate of righteousness, and, as shoes for your feet, having put on the readiness given by the gospel of peace. In all circumstances take up the shield of faith, with which you can extinguish all the flaming darts of the evil one; and take the helmet of salvation, and the sword of the Spirit, which is the word of God..."

(Ephesians 6:14-17, ESV)

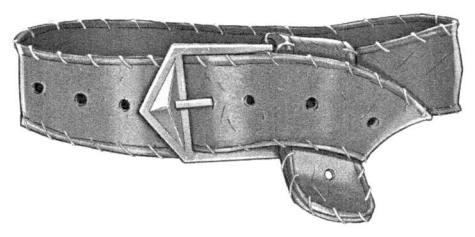

1
THE BELT OF TRUTH

"Stand therefore, having fastened on the belt of truth..." Ephesians 6:14

What does Paul mean by "truth" here?

Truth is what corresponds to reality, agrees with the facts, or the way things really are. For example, if I said "I have a cat as a pet" it would not be true because it can't be supported with reality. Right now, the fact that I have a pet dog is reality.

Also, God is the Author of truth, therefore the truth is whatever agrees with His words. Jesus said, *"I am the Way, the Truth, and the Life."* (John 14:6)

Remember, Satan's tactics are to deceive us and convince us to create our own truth. Knowing God's truth well is key to combating this tactic!

Why is the belt of truth listed first? It is the foundation of all the rest of the armor. If there is no such thing as truth, there can be no righteousness, good news, faith, salvation, or word of God!

How can we practically put on truth like a belt?

To practically wear the belt is to always be a passionate seeker and advocate of the TRUTH!

There are a lot of doctrines out there today, or what people like to call their personal "truths". We need to know how to rightly divide the word of truth and be on guard, which means we know how to recognize truth from error.

Ephesians 4:14-15 *"We should no longer be children, tossed to and fro and carried about with every wind of doctrine, by the trickery of men, in the cunning craftiness of deceitful plotting,* (there are Satan's tactics again) *but, speaking the truth in love, may grow up in all things into Him who is the head – Christ"*.

2 Tim. 2:15 *"Be diligent to present yourself approved to God, a worker who does not need to be*

ashamed, rightly dividing the word of truth."

God's truth is found in the Bible. We need to know it to live in a way that is pleasing to God and to fight the tactics of the enemy!

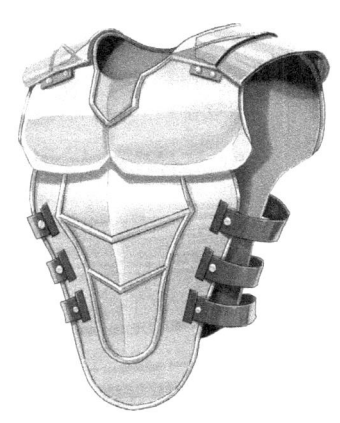

2
BREASTPLATE OF RIGHTEOUSNESS

"...having put on the breastplate of righteousness..." Ephesians 6:14

Righteousness is being determined innocent, just, or holy. Remember, God says in Leviticus 11:44 to be holy as He is holy. How are we supposed to do that when we are born sinners?

But God. Isaiah 1:18 says, *"though your sins are like scarlet, they shall be as white as snow."* How?

Romans 3:21-26 *"But now the righteousness of God has been [made real] apart from the law ... through faith in Jesus Christ for all who believe. For there is no distinction: for all have sinned and fall short of the glory of God, and are justified by his grace as a gift, through the redemption that is in Christ Jesus, whom God put forward as a [satisfaction] by his blood, to be received by faith. This was to show God's righteousness, because in his divine forbearance he had passed over former sins. It was to show his righteousness at the present time, so that he might be just and the justifier of the one who has faith in Jesus."*

So even though we are all guilty of sin, we were ratified, or made officially, holy through the shed blood of Jesus Christ on the cross. God is not only the Judge, He sent His Son to pay for our sin, and sealed us that way for eternity. All we have to do is place our faith in Jesus to receive it.

Putting on God's righteousness is the idea of a jury looking you over, KNOWING you are guilty, and judging you as innocent, simply because they aren't seeing you anymore, they are seeing Him. How?

2 Cor. 5:21 *"For our sake He made Him to be sin who knew no sin, so that in Him we might become the righteousness of God."* They are seeing Him instead because we are to put on HIS RIGHTEOUSNESS instead. Our own righteousness is as filthy rags, and cannot save us.

Romans 8:33-34 *"Who shall bring any charge against God's elect? It is God who justifies. Who is to condemn? Christ Jesus is the One who died — more than that, who was raised — who is at the right hand of God, who indeed is interceding for us."*

That is why our armor is effective: because Jesus is alive, and still fighting for its durability and reliability. He is our quality control. He determines how sturdy our armor is, and since He is God, we can trust Him, and it.

What does it mean practically to put on the breastplate of righteousness?

It means that you should be making no provision for your flesh (giving into it) and should no longer be returning to the well of the world to satisfy your flesh. Romans 13:14 says, *"But put on the Lord Jesus Christ, and make no provision for the flesh, to gratify its desires."*

Do not feed your flesh! Don't throw what Jesus did for you back in His face. Now, does this mean you need to be perfect? No, we are humans, it's not possible for us to be perfect in our own power. But we can live out through the Holy Spirit what we are: a new creation.

2 Cor. 5:17 *"Therefore, if anyone is in Christ, he is a new creation. The old has passed away; behold, the new has come."*

In Lev. 11:44 where it says, "Be holy as I am holy", did you know it also tells us how to do that?

"Consecrate yourselves (be set apart) and don't defile yourself." Be set apart from the world and don't allow Satan to get a foothold, even in the small things!

Romans 12:2 says, *"Do not conform to the pattern of this world, but be transformed by the renewing of your mind. Then you will be able to test and approve what God's will is – His good, pleasing and perfect will."*

It is a choice you make everyday whether to live like Christ and please God, or to live like the world. It's up to you. One is righteous, one is not, but it's ultimately your choice whether or not to put on the armor.

3
SHOES OF READINESS

"...as shoes for your feet, having put on the readiness given by the gospel of peace..."
Ephesians 6:15

This means that you *"concentrate on being completely devoted to Christ in your hearts. Be ready at any time to give a quiet and reverent answer to any man who wants a reason for the hope that you have within you"* (1 Peter 3:15, Phillips)

If you study to show yourself approved, and know your Bible well enough to not be deceived by Satan twisting it, you're off to a good start to being ready to share the gospel with those you come into contact with.

Remember, **every interaction is a chance for action.**

Every time you interact with someone, you never know what that conversation could turn into, so be ready. You need to be able to think on your feet! In the world we live in today though, sometimes that means being able to do more than just rattle off some verses you memorized from the Bible. We live in a world where people don't accept the Bible as truth, so sometimes you first have to give the case for why the Bible is true, or why we know Jesus was a real person and that the evidence points to the fact that He rose from the dead. This is what is known as "apologetic evangelism" which is giving the case for why Christianity is true.

Why should we expect people to believe in Christianity if they don't have good reasons for believing it is true?

<u>What does it mean to have shoes of readiness?</u>

Always be ready to give an answer for the hope that is in you and be able to tell them *why* it is the truth! People need the Prince of Peace in this crazy, chaotic world. Be ready to tell them about Him!

Rom. 10:15 *"How beautiful are the feet of those who preach the gospel of peace, who bring glad tidings of good things!"*

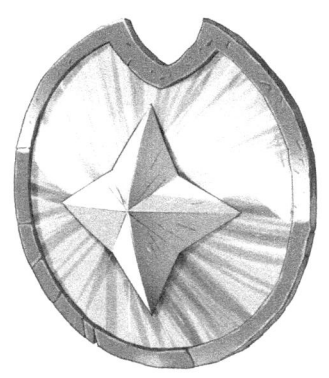

4
SHIELD OF FAITH

*"In all circumstances take up the shield of faith,
with which you can extinguish all the flaming
darts of the evil one..."* Ephesians 6:16

Wait, I'm sorry, what? Now he is shooting
fiery darts at us? Wasn't this supposed to be
an invisible war? And if so, what are these
flaming darts? As a theologian, I couldn't
come up with much about them. So I started
thinking about it as a history teacher. This was
written during the ancient Roman empire, and
Paul is thinking about a specific tactic that was
utilized by the enemies of Rome, and using
it as an analogy for Satan's spiritual tactics
against us.

In all my study about how Rome fell, I can tell you they had no shortage of enemies, from all different cultures (the Huns, the Visigoths, the Vandals, etc.) and therefore, had to be ready for any tactic that came their way.

They had a couple ways of defending against these fiery arrows:

First, they would use metal in their shields, instead of just wood, so the fire wouldn't set it ablaze, thus rendering it useless. This meant their shield was strong and sturdy. Just like your faith needs to be. Speaking of, let's talk about faith for a minute. What does the Bible say about the strength of faith?

Heb. 11:1-3 says, *"Now faith is the assurance of things hoped for, the conviction of things not seen... By faith we understand that the universe was created by the word of God, so that what is visible was made out of things that are invisible."*

So, faith is having trust that the hope offered by an invisible God is real and will eventually come to pass, and also trusting that what we see is made up of things we don't see. Aside from the scientific explanation given for atoms here, there is another point to make. People will try to tell you that as a Christian, you are dumb to have faith in an invisible God. But to be honest, there is not one human alive who doesn't exercise faith in the unseen on a daily basis. For example, before sitting down to read this, did any one of you verify the durability of your chair by calling the engineer who designed it? No. Neither does an Atheist. He just trusts that the chair will hold him because he sees the effect of the design (the chair itself). Just like we can see the effects of the design of the universe. And if there is design, by logic, there must be an all-powerful Designer.

In Matthew 17:20-21, Jesus cures a boy from possession by an evil spirit after the disciples were unable to. Afterwards they ask him why they couldn't. He responded,

"I assure you that if you have as much faith as a grain of mustard-seed you can say to this hill, 'Up you get and move over there!' and it will move — you will find nothing is impossible. However, this kind does not go out except by prayer and fasting"

So if your faith is strong enough, you can do the impossible. But, some things are beyond our abilities and we need to humble ourselves and ask for some help. That is where prayer and fasting come in.

Matthew 21:21-22 says, *"'Believe me,' replied Jesus, 'if you have faith and have no doubts in your heart, ...if you should say to this hill, "Get up and throw yourself into the sea", it will happen!*

Everything you ask for in prayer, if you have faith, you will receive.'"

Again, faith and prayer go together! Why? Because faith is tested by how healthy your prayer life is. If you don't pray because you don't believe Someone is there and listening, or trust that the answer given is the right one, then your faith is too small.

Hebrews 11:6 says, *"And without faith it is impossible to please Him, for whoever would draw near to God must believe that He exists and that He rewards those who seek Him."*

How do you practically take up the shield of faith?

Just like the metal material the Romans made their shields out of, your faith needs to be strong and sturdy, strengthened through time spent in prayer. Faithful prayer pleases God. It is a sweet aroma to Him, (Exodus 30). In Psalm 141:2, David writes, *"May my prayer be set before you like incense."* In Revelation (5:8, 8:3-4), it says that our prayers ascend to heaven like incense and that God collects our prayers like incense in golden bowls.

Why? Because prayer reflects our trust and confidence in Him. We pray because we DO believe Someone is there, and that He is listening and cares about us. Prayer is an outward expression and strengthening of our faith.

Second, the arrows that the enemy sends are cut off, before they can catch the soldier on fire. A defensive strategy is to recognize the danger of the fire and CUT OFF or stop Satan before his attack has a chance to burn you!

In the Garden, Eve should have been like, "Wait what? I don't remember wanting to be like God. I was just here minding my own business when you rolled up and told me that was what I wanted. No thanks, serpent, you can just make your way back to wherever you came from."

Remember, Satan is using you to get to God, meaning he will try and convince you that you want things that you never even thought about wanting before. Because his goal is to stick it to God by using you to hurt Him. Don't let him get away with it!

James 4:7 says *"Resist the devil and he will flee from you!"* Tell him to take a hike out of your life!

Genesis 4:7 says, *"Sin is lurking at the door; and its desire is for you, but you must master it."*

That means CUT IT OUT of your life. It may be habit you need to give up, or a relationship that you need to cut off, but if you don't, your faith will always be hindered.

Hebrews 12:1b-2a says, *"Let us throw off* [get rid of] *everything that hinders and the sin that so easily entangles. And let us run with perseverance the race marked out for us, fixing our eyes on Jesus, the Pioneer and Perfecter of faith."*

5
HELMET OF SALVATION

"…take the helmet of salvation…" Ephesians 6:17

The theological definition of salvation is "deliverance from sin and its consequences, brought about by faith in Christ." That's why it comes after the shield of faith. There is no salvation apart from faith! Ephesians 2:8 says, *"For by grace you have been saved **through** faith."*

Why did Paul use the helmet as a picture of salvation? Well, there's precedence in Scripture for it.

Psalm 140:7 *"O God the Lord, the strength of my salvation, You have covered my head in the day of battle."*

Is. 59:17 *"For He put on righteousness as a breastplate, And a helmet of salvation on His head."*

However, I think it is coupled with the helmet because of how important the helmet is in battle. Or, think about sports for a minute. Any type of sport where there is a good chance of getting a head injury, it requires the athletes to wear a helmet. Why? Because while you can get beaned in the arm or the leg with a fastball and live, there's a chance of death if it hits you hard enough in the head.

The helmet protects the most vulnerable and most important part of you. So does salvation. Unless you are saved, the rest of the armor doesn't matter because you haven't activated what makes it effective: the supernatural power of the Holy Spirit. Just like in football, if you aren't wearing a helmet when you get tackled at full speed, those leg pads will do nothing for your head if you hit it hard enough. You need to be covered head to toe, especially the head!

If you have salvation through faith, you need fear nothing, you have access to God's entire army!

Psalm 27:1 *"The Lord is my light and my salvation; Whom shall I fear?"*

Ps. 62:2 *"He only is my rock and my salvation; He is my defense; I shall not be greatly moved."*

If you're saved, you got this!

Always remember…

 "He who is in you is greater than he who is in the world" 1 Jn. 4:4

Jesus said, *"Behold, I give you the authority to trample on serpents and scorpions, and over all the power of the enemy, and nothing shall by any means hurt you."* Luke 10:19

James says, *"Even the demons believe – and tremble!"* Jas. 2:19

How can we be protected by this helmet of salvation?

Well first, it says to literally "take" it.

See, salvation is a free gift, but God isn't going to force it on anyone. He doesn't want God-loving robots because forced love isn't true love. He gave us free will, and it is up to us to receive or "take" this free gift for ourselves. He is not going to force us to spend eternity with Him if we don't want to. As C.S. Lewis said, God is not going to drag us kicking and screaming into heaven. If you don't want it, you will get exactly what you do want: an eternity spent apart from Him. But remember, He is the source of all of the goodness, love, and light in this world, so before you reject Him, consider what that eternity without those things will be like.

If you do want His gift of salvation, "take" it up by praying to God, and asking Him for it by placing your faith in Jesus Christ.

Romans 10:9 says, "*If you confess with your mouth that Jesus is Lord and believe in your heart that God raised Him from the dead, you will be saved.*"

Second, if you have it already, REMIND yourself you have it! And with it, access to the riches and power of Christ Jesus!

"*He has delivered us from the power of darkness and conveyed us into the kingdom of the Son of His love, in whom we have redemption through His blood, the forgiveness of sins.*" Colossians 1:13-14

"*There is therefore now no condemnation to those who are in Christ Jesus, who do not walk according to the flesh, but according to the Spirit. For the law of the Spirit of life in Christ Jesus has made me free from the law of sin and death.*" Romans 8:1-2

When Satan tries to remind you of your past, be sure to remind him of his future. And remind him that you have the power of the Almighty God on your side, so he better get ready because the host of heaven is coming for him!

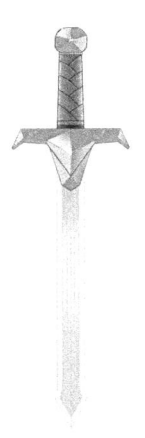

6
SWORD OF THE SPIRIT

"...and the sword of the Spirit, which is the word of God..." Ephesians 6:17

The Bible is depicted as a sword here. Why?

Hebrews 4:12 says, *"For the word of God is living and active, sharper than any two-edged sword, piercing to the division of soul and of spirit, of joints and of marrow, and discerning the thoughts and intentions of the heart."*

The word of God has the power to change lives! It can convict or encourage, which is something humans need--on a daily basis.

How can we practically wield the sword of the spirit?

KNOW IT, and Know it well!

Remember what happened when Jesus was being tempted by Satan in the desert? He cut him to the quick [no pun intended] using Scripture! Same thing happened when the Pharisees came after him in Matthew 9.

The word of God is a two-edged sword in that it is both a defensive (protective) weapon that can deflect blows as we mentioned Jesus did, but it is also an offensive one. You can use it to defeat Satan's plans by sharing it with others! However, in order to wield it, you must know it! Remember what 2 Timothy 2:15 said: study to show yourself approved and be able to rightly divide the word of truth!

"All Scripture is breathed out by God and profitable for teaching, for reproof, for correction, and for training in righteousness, that the [hu]man of God may be complete, equipped for every good work." 2 Tim. 3:16-17

The Bible also says God has given us everything we need to be successful in this battle! *"His divine power has given us everything required for life and godliness through the knowledge of Him who called us by His own glory and goodness."* 2 Peter 1:3

7 & 8
CLOAK OF ZEAL
AND
POSTURE OF PRAYER

Finally, Ephesians 6:18-20 wraps up and says,

"Praying at all times in the Spirit, with all prayer and supplication. To that end, keep alert with all perseverance, making supplication for all the saints, and also for me, that words may be given to me in opening my mouth boldly to proclaim the mystery of the gospel, for which I am an ambassador in chains, that I may declare it boldly, as I ought to speak."

Prayer and zeal in sharing the gospel are the other offensive weapons besides the word of

God. I like to think of them as the honorary seventh and eighth pieces of armor.

In Isaiah 59:17, after talking about the helmet and breastplate, the prophet mentions a warrior who wraps himself in zeal as a cloak.

Zeal can be defined as passion, intensity, or enthusiasm. It is the state of having urgent love for something. To effectively share the Gospel with people, you need to have an urgent love of humans. If you don't care about people, you will be apathetic about sharing the Gospel with them.

Zeal leads to boldness because devotion to sharing the Gospel can overcome any fear you may have in entering a situation.

In 1 Thessalonians 2:2, Paul writes, "*You know how badly we had been treated at Philippi just before we came to you and how much we suffered there. Yet our God gave us the courage to declare His good news to you boldly, in spite of great opposition.*" Also, in Philippians 1:14, he writes, "*…because of my imprisonment, most of the believers here have gained confidence and boldly speak God's message without fear.*"

"*Since this new [covenant] gives us such confidence, we can be very bold.*" 2 Cor. 3:12

"*For God has not given us a spirit of fear, but of*

power and of love and of a sound mind. Therefore, do not be ashamed of the testimony of our Lord…" 2 Tim. 1:7-8

Finally, the warrior's heart needs to have a posture of prayer to truly have victory in this spiritual battle. Notice there is no physical posture mentioned: it has to do with the motivation of the heart. Throughout Scripture, people prayed in many different kinds of posture: standing, sitting, kneeling, laying facedown on the ground, and not one was superior to another. The position of your body doesn't matter as much as the position of your heart. As mentioned before in the chapter on faith, prayer is evidence that you trust God and His will in all things.

1 John 5:14 says, *"Now this is the confidence that we have in Him, that if we ask anything according to His will, He hears us."*

"Let us therefore come boldly to the throne of grace, that we may obtain mercy and find grace to help in time of need." Hebrews 4:16

Remember in Mark 9:29, Jesus said to his disciples, *"This kind* [of evil spirit] *cannot be driven out by anything but prayer."*

Prayer is necessary to be effective in this spiritual battle––do not neglect it! They say to fight fire with fire, so make sure to fight spirit with Spirit!

James tells us that, *"The effective, fervent prayer of a righteous man avails much."* (Jas. 5:16)

How do you practically put on the cloak of zeal and have a posture of prayer?

Understand that God calls every believer (not just professional missionaries) to make disciples of all nations, (Mt. 28:19). First, pray and ask God to give you a love for all people and their spiritual state. Second, do a study on the effectiveness of fasting as a spiritual discipline, and then apply it to your life. Lastly, pray for boldness and confidence when opportunities arise to share the Gospel. You never know when God may open a door for you to wield the Sword of the Spirit!

CONCLUSION

God has endowed you with free will. No one is going to force you to put this spiritual armor on, it's your choice. But just know if you don't, there are two outcomes: If you step out in service to God, you will be on Satan's radar, and you will have no defensive protection from a very real spiritual battle that is happening around you. You WILL take a beating and lose.

Or, you will be so ineffective for God's Kingdom that Satan won't care about you and leave you alone, and you will still lose because he will continue to rule this world unopposed and culture will just continue to get worse.

But God provides a third option where you take a stand. You step out, put on the armor everyday, and WIN the battle. It's up to you.

I would like to leave you with a quote about spiritual warfare from Elizabeth Jane Whately, who is the subject of an upcoming book in my women in historical apologetics series. In 1875, she wrote a book entitled, *How to Answer Objections to Revealed Religion*. This was in the Introduction:

"In a well-disciplined army, the officers are not only trained to handle arms and resist an attack from the enemy, but are instructed in the most efficient and successful modes of laying siege to fortresses, defending important stations from assailants, and, in short, are prepared in every way to meet any plans that may be laid against them.

We have to deal with an unsleeping, ever-ready antagonist––one who knows every inch of the battleground, and has an eagle eye to spy out our weak points. Do we meet him prepared as we should be for the battle?

…Our plain duty is to be prepared to meet the devices and snares which the enemy of our souls is ever on the watch to plan against us.

At the present day, he appears to be peculiarly active in trying to shake men's faith in [supernatural] religion. There has been no lack of attempts of this kind ever since Christianity was first preached; but in our age this anti-Christian spirit seems to be pervading all classes of society and almost every department of literature. Many scientific men are sparing no pains in trying to turn the knowledge they have acquired into weapons against the revelation of Him who is the Author of Nature.

…In every walk of life, we are [likely] to [interact] with those who will bring forward objections against the truth of Christianity. It is no use to shut our eyes and ears to this state of things and to [imagine] we shall be safe by ignoring it. The only security is to be well-prepared beforehand. True, no study and no reasoning power will supply the place of a heart truly taught by the Spirit of God, and of a humble [...] mind, such as only the influence of [the] Spirit can give. But our part is to be armed on all sides; and it is surely [a duty for all] to seek to be 'ready always to give an answer to every man that asks you a reason of the hope that is in you.' (1 Pet. 3:15)

...When the adversary meets us, we are plainly called on by our [Lord] to be ready, as soldiers of Christ, with 'the shield of faith and the sword of the Spirit,' to repel his attacks; and to be rightly able to do this we must be on our guard [...] and ourselves prepared when the call comes to defend the Lord's cause, in His strength."

APPENDIX

"Grow Through What You Go Through"

TRIALS AS TRAINING

While the point of the book of Job is not to explain why we go through trials, there are a few insights we can pick up as an outside observer to Job's pain:

As a believer, suffering on this Earth is not a punishment. On the contrary, being tested is a reward for faithfulness. "Trials and suffering are for our education and training. The athlete is not put under strict discipline as a punishment, but to make him ready for the race. Christ is ever preparing us for the race that is set before us...In this case, Job was being honored by God. God knew He could trust Job to remain faithful to Him in spite of everything," (Henrietta Mears, *What the Bible is All About*, "Job").

James 1:2-4 says, *"Consider it pure joy, my brothers and sisters, whenever you face trials of many kinds, because you know that the testing of your faith produces perseverance. Let perseverance finish its work so that you may be mature and complete, not lacking anything."* As the saying goes: "Grow through what you go through." In times of severe testing, we should not ask

"*How* can I get out of this?" but "*What* can I get out of this?" We are to endure AND mature through the trials that God allows.

GROWTH POTENTIAL

There are a few specific areas of our lives that trials are specifically suited to help us grow:

1. <u>Humility</u>:

Job was upright, but he knew it. He was self-righteous. In Job 29:1-25, he focuses on himself, using personal pronouns 52x. Believers are allowed to suffer to bring us to the end of ourselves, so God can be the One to lift us up. We need to realize that God is the only One who can "fix" what is broken, that we do not have the power in and of ourselves to do so. God uses suffering for our good and for *His* glory. Job begged throughout the book for an audience with God to be able to plead his case––that he was righteous and did not deserve suffering––yet when he was finally faced with the glory of God, Job realized he was the one who needed to repent.

2. <u>Character Development</u>:

Romans 8:28-29 says, "*And we know that all things work together for good to those who love God, to those who are the called according to His purpose. For whom He foreknew, He also* predestined to be conformed to the image of His Son..." As believers, we are being conformed to the image of Jesus Christ. Jesus' whole reason for coming to Earth was to suffer. We are also tried by fire, in order to reveal the gold within. Job 23:10 says, *"But He knows the way that I take and when He has tested me, I shall come forth as gold."* However, Job knew this was only an effect of certain causes. He knew that to come forth like gold, there was some responsibility on his part to abide in the Vine. Which leads us to...

3.   Intimacy with God:

Job's responsibility was to abide in God alone. Verses 11-12 in Job 23 continue to say, *"My feet have closely followed His steps; I have kept to His way without turning aside. I have not departed from the commands of His lips; I have treasured the words of His mouth more than my daily bread."* How often do we spend time with God when things are good? And then how quickly do we run to Him when things are difficult? Sometimes God allows us to go through trials to bring us closer to Himself. John 15 says, *"Remain in Me, as I also remain in you. No branch can bear fruit by itself; it must remain in the vine. Neither can you bear fruit unless you remain in Me...If you keep My commands, you will remain in My love, just as I have kept My Father's commands and remain in His love. I have told you this so that*

My joy may be in you and that your joy may be complete."

4.   Preparation to comfort others:

The last area that we have potential to grow in is our ability to comfort others. 2 Corinthians 1:3-4 says, *"Praise be to…the Father of compassion and the God of all comfort, who comforts us in all our troubles, so that we can comfort those in any trouble with the comfort we ourselves receive from God."* God is not only training us to endure, but to also come alongside others and help them endure. Often, when we are going through something, God brings us through it only to have us later come into contact with someone who is going through something similar. We are then able to speak into their lives and counsel them more effectively than if we had no idea what they were going through. Heb. 4:15 says, *"For we do not have a High Priest who is unable to empathize with our weaknesses, but we have one who has been tempted in every way, just as we are – yet He did not sin."* We need to follow Christ's example: exhibit empathy and encourage those who are suffering not to sin in their anguish. Satan will be right there whispering in their ear that God is to blame for their hurt and that it would be better if they turned their backs on Him. Let it not be so.

SARAHRENTERLINE.COM

 **@sarahrenterline**

Sarah is an author, apologist, pastor's wife, mother, and teacher. She has undergraduate degrees in Biblical Studies, Christian Studies (Theology and Ministry), Social and Behavioral Science, and Philosophy; a CA State Credential in teaching History; and an M.A. in Christian Leadership.

From 2009 – 2016, she was the President of The International Society of Women in Apologetics and was also a writer and editor on the Special Divine Action Project for Oxford University. She is currently working as an apologist and writer with the Library of Historical Apologetics.

She has taught Apologetics, Biblical Studies, Philosophy, and History at both the secondary and college levels. She also speaks at churches and conferences around the country, and has frequently guested on numerous radio shows and podcasts. Sarah is married to Matt, a Pastor and the Co-Director of Calvary Curriculum and Calvary Posters. They have two sons, Lochlann and Declan.

She currently has four books published, including *A Visual Guide to Biblical Apologetics* for Harvest House Publishers and is currently hard at work on a fifth book about women in historical apologetics tentatively titled, *Modern Women: The Forgotten Female Apologists of the Modern Era.*

CHECK OUT SARAH'S OTHER BOOKS

No Apologies: The Life and Work of Susanna Newcome

Digging Deeper: The Life and Work of Mary Brodrick

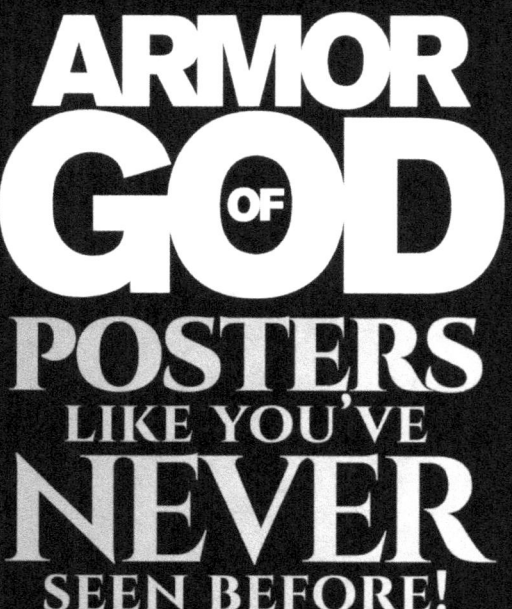

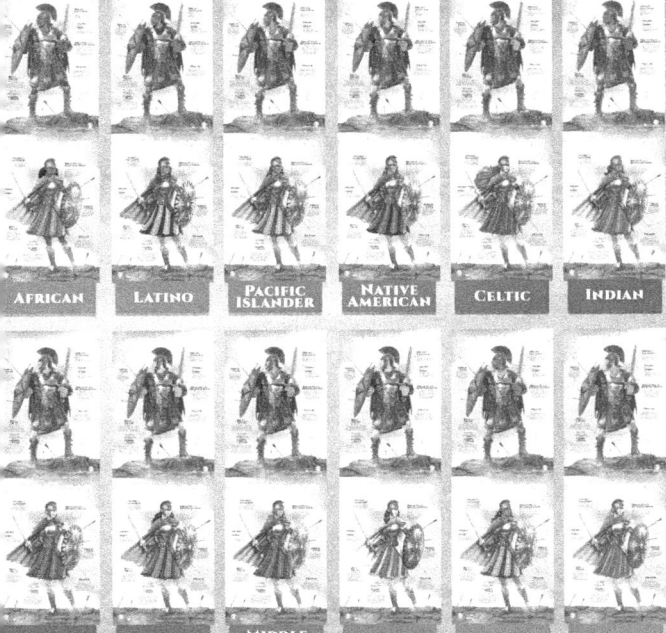

www.ingramcontent.com/pod-product-compliance
Lightning Source LLC
Chambersburg PA
CBHW060347130626
46553CB00003B/1124